MAKE it WORK!

FLIGHT

Andrew Haslam

written by
Jack Challoner

Photography: Jon Barnes
Consultant: Graham Peacock
Senior Lecturer in Science Education at
Sheffield Hallam University

TWO-CAN
in association with
WATTS BOOKS

MAKE it WORK!
Other titles

Body
Building
Earth
Electricity
Insects
Machines
Plants
Sound
Space

First published in Great Britain in 1995 by
Two-Can Publishing Ltd
346 Old Street
London EC1V 9NQ
in association with
Watts Books
96 Leonard Street
London EC2A 4RH

Printed and bound in Hong Kong

Hardback 2 4 6 8 10 9 7 5 3 1
Paperback 2 4 6 8 10 9 7 5 3 1

A catalogue record for this book is available
from the British Library.

Hardback ISBN: 1 85434 317 3
Paperback ISBN: 1 85434 332 7

Series Editor: Kate Asser
Editor: Dr Kathryn Senior
Series concept and design: Andrew Haslam and Wendy Baker
Designer: Peter Clayman

Thanks also to: Cordel Eliss, Rachel and Jonathon Bee,
and everyone at Plough Studios

Contents

Words marked in **bold** in the
text are explained in the glossary.

Being an Engineer

Today, there are many different flying machines. There are aeroplanes, gliders, hot-air balloons, airships and even rockets that fly beyond the **atmosphere**. But how did we learn to fly? And how does a heavy aeroplane stay in the air?

Building different aircraft

Aeroplanes are designed for different uses. Fighter jets must be fast and easy to manoeuvre, while aeroplanes that carry passengers need to be safe and comfortable. The materials used to build aeroplanes have different abilities, too. Most parts need to be strong and light, some parts need to bend, while others have to cope with intense heat.

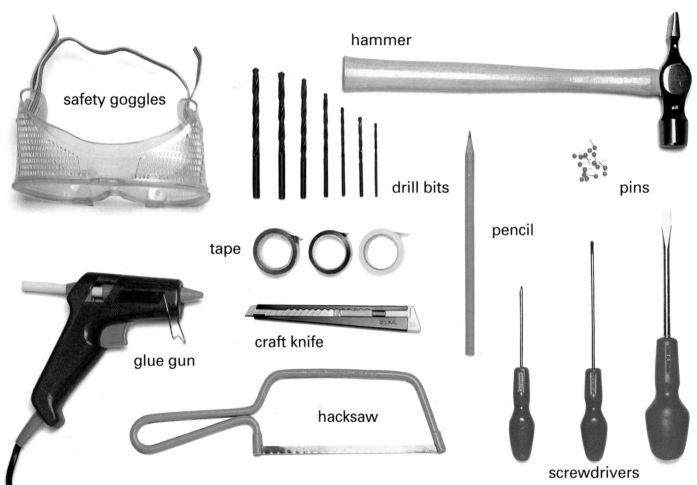

safety goggles

hammer

drill bits

pins

pencil

tape

glue gun

craft knife

hacksaw

screwdrivers

Four **forces** act on any flying object. **Gravity** pulls an aircraft down towards the earth. Wings produce **lift**, which works upwards against gravity as the aircraft moves in the air. A third force, **thrust**, pushes an aircraft forwards and **drag**, or **air resistance**, slows it down. To get an object airborne, lift and thrust have to overcome gravity and drag.

MAKE it WORK!

You don't need to build aeroplanes that fly at **supersonic** speeds to learn more about flight. The projects in this book show you how to make different types of flying models and reveal the secrets of how they stay in the air. Many of the projects concentrate on aeroplanes, but other things fly, too. By making a boomerang, an arrow, a Frisbee, a rotor and even a powerful rocket, you will see that some things stay in the air more easily than others.

You will need

For each project you will find a list of the things you need to make the model. Most materials can be found around the home. Cardboard tubes, paperclips, string, card and cotton reels are often needed. You may also need to visit the shops. Balsa wood is very useful for making flying models as it is both strong and light. You will also need a few basic tools. Some of the equipment shown below will come in handy for many of the projects.

Drilling

For some of the projects in this book you will need to drill holes. Use a pointed bradawl to start the holes and finish them off with a hand drill. This stops the drill bit from sliding about. Make sure that the bit is the correct size.

Joining

A glue stick used with a glue gun is an easy way to join parts of your model together. Let the glue dry before carrying out test flights.

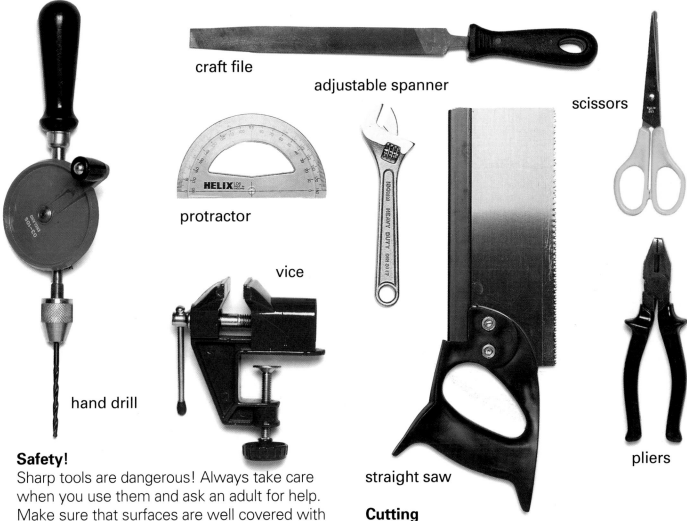

craft file

adjustable spanner

scissors

protractor

vice

hand drill

straight saw

pliers

Safety!

Sharp tools are dangerous! Always take care when you use them and ask an adult for help. Make sure that surfaces are well covered with old newspaper. If you want to cut or drill wood, use a small table vice to hold the pieces firmly, so that they do not slip.

Planning

Always plan projects before you start. Read the instructions carefully and take a close look at the photographs.

Cutting

You will need a saw for cutting wood, and scissors for cutting card and paper. A craft knife is useful too, but it is better if you ask an adult to cut things for you as it has a sharp blade. Measure each part accurately before cutting and always cut away from your fingers. You can smooth over rough edges of wood or polystyrene with sandpaper or a file.

Many years ago, some scientists used photographs of birds in flight to help them understand how birds fly. They found that it was the movement and shape of birds' wings that made flight possible. The feathers at the wing tips produce thrust, pushing the bird through the air. The wing shape means that lift is produced as air moves over it.

1 Use a compass to draw two circles with a **radius** of 12 cm each. Draw one circle on corrugated cardboard and the other on paper.

2 Mark the centres of the circles and then cut them out carefully.

3 Using a protractor, mark the outlines of 10 equally spaced slits (they should be 36° apart), on the paper disc. Your disc should look like the one shown below. Do the same again for the cardboard circle.

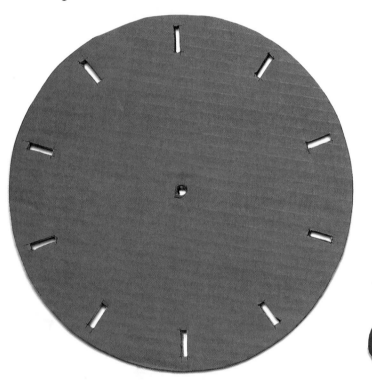

MAKE it WORK!

A spinning disc called a **phenakistoscope** will make a series of drawings appear as a moving picture. You can use a phenakistoscope to study how birds move their wings in flight.

You will need

a pen	Plasticine
paper	paper glue
scissors	a craft knife
a compass	a large mirror
a protractor	wooden dowel
corrugated cardboard	old newspapers

3 Put a thick layer of old newspaper over your table or desk top to protect it. Ask an adult to help you cut out 10 slits in both discs, 3 cm long x 0.5 cm wide, with a craft knife.

4 Leave the cardboard disc to one side. Copy the 10 bird drawings shown, above left, as accurately as you can on to the paper disc, beneath each slit.

5 Line up the slits in both the discs so that you can see through them. Glue the paper disc to the cardboard disc, plain side down.

6 Make a hole through the centre of both discs and push the dowel through. Secure the dowel with a lump of Plasticine.

7 Stand the mirror up and sit in front of it. Hold your phenakistoscope in front of the mirror, as shown. Look through the slits from behind and turn the dowel in your fingers. You should be able to see a bird in flight.

For hundreds of years people tried to copy the motion of flying birds. They attached wings to themselves and flapped as hard as they could. But all their attempts failed. Humans would have to have much stronger muscles and much lighter bodies to be able to fly like birds.

Just as a spinning top will not topple as long as it stays spinning, so the spin of a boomerang or a Frisbee gives it **stability** in the air. When you throw a Frisbee, it is launched with its front edge higher than its back edge. This produces lift which helps it to stay in the air longer. A boomerang's spin and curved shape cause it to change direction as it flies.

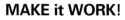

MAKE it WORK!
See if you can find the best way of launching your own Frisbee and boomerang.

To make a Frisbee you will need
an aluminium pie dish   Plasticine

1 Press three small balls of Plasticine on to the outside edge of the dish at equal distances apart.

2 Launch your Frisbee with one hand, as shown above. As you release it, flick your wrist forwards to make the Frisbee spin. Does it fly better with a fast or slow spin?

Boomerangs have been used by Aborigines in Australia for 10,000 years. They were mainly used for hunting and as weapons. The oldest known boomerang was found in Poland and is about 20,000 years old. Today, boomerangs are used for sport.

To make a boomerang you will need

stiff card   a 12 cm x 4 cm block of wood
a craft knife   wooden dowel or a pencil

1 Copy the shape of the boomerang shown above on to the card (each side is 15 cm long). Ask an adult to help cut it out with a craft knife.

2 Hold the wooden block in one hand and place the boomerang on top of it, as shown below. Take hold of the wooden dowel or pencil in your other hand.

3 To launch your boomerang, hit it hard at one end in a forward motion with the dowel or pencil. Your boomerang will turn as it flies.

The bow and arrow has been used for over 30,000 years as a fast and accurate hunting weapon. The flight at the end of an arrow is vital to its accuracy, as it helps it to fly straight. As soon as an arrow is released from a bow, it is slowed down by air resistance. The faster an arrow moves, the further it travels before hitting the ground. As arrows are long and straight, drag is reduced.

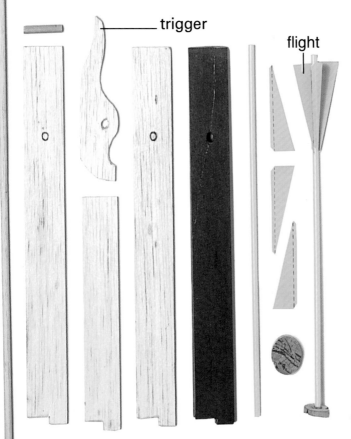

trigger

flight

MAKE it WORK!

This crossbow uses **energy** from muscles in the archer's arm to make arrows fly. As the bowstring is pulled back, energy from muscles in the arm transfers to the **strained** bow. This stored energy makes the arrow shoot forwards when the string is released. Make your own crossbow and find out how flights affect the accuracy of arrows.

You will need

glue	a hand drill
string	balsa wood
a cork	a craft knife
a saw	wooden dowel
a straw	a sewing needle
thin card	

1 Carefully cut a wooden dowel about 80 cm long. Tie 1 m of string to the dowel at both ends, as shown left, to make a bow.

2 To make the handle, cut two pieces of balsa wood 30 cm x 5 cm, and 18 cm x 4.5 cm. Make a notch in one end of each piece, as shown left. Cut out another piece 12 cm long for the trigger.

3 Drill holes through the handle pieces and trigger. Make them big enough to allow a short wooden dowel to slot through.

4 Line up the notched ends of the balsa wood pieces. Glue them together with the 18 cm piece in the middle and leave to dry.

5 Slot the trigger in between the long pieces of balsa wood. Line up the holes and put in the dowel.

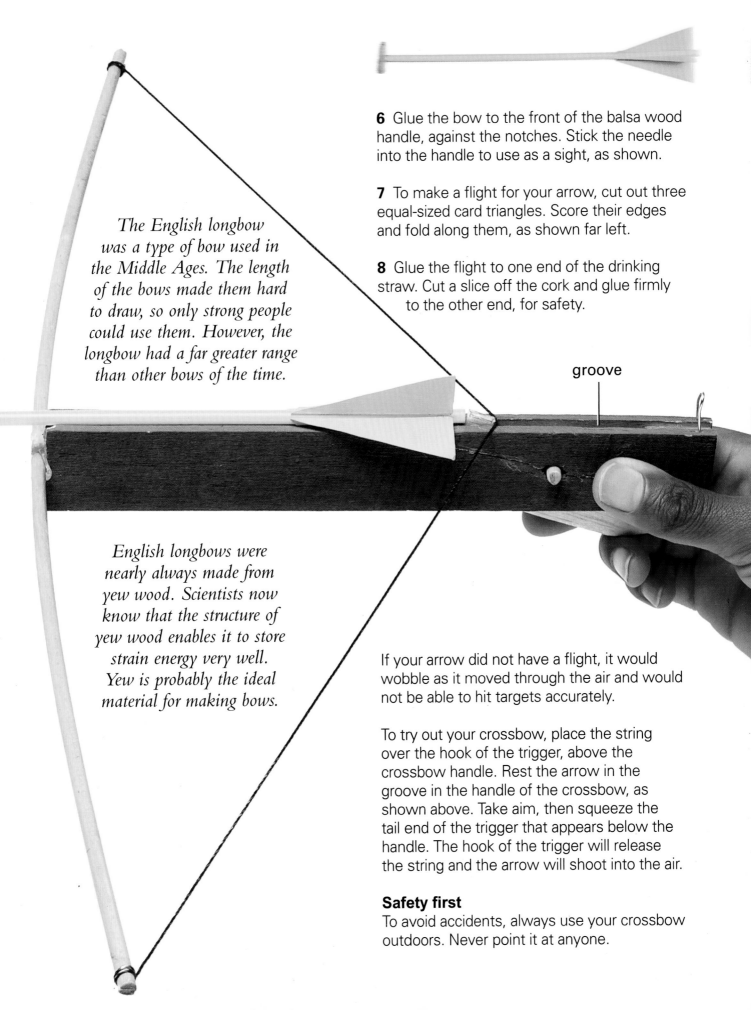

The English longbow was a type of bow used in the Middle Ages. The length of the bows made them hard to draw, so only strong people could use them. However, the longbow had a far greater range than other bows of the time.

English longbows were nearly always made from yew wood. Scientists now know that the structure of yew wood enables it to store strain energy very well. Yew is probably the ideal material for making bows.

6 Glue the bow to the front of the balsa wood handle, against the notches. Stick the needle into the handle to use as a sight, as shown.

7 To make a flight for your arrow, cut out three equal-sized card triangles. Score their edges and fold along them, as shown far left.

8 Glue the flight to one end of the drinking straw. Cut a slice off the cork and glue firmly to the other end, for safety.

groove

If your arrow did not have a flight, it would wobble as it moved through the air and would not be able to hit targets accurately.

To try out your crossbow, place the string over the hook of the trigger, above the crossbow handle. Rest the arrow in the groove in the handle of the crossbow, as shown above. Take aim, then squeeze the tail end of the trigger that appears below the handle. The hook of the trigger will release the string and the arrow will shoot into the air.

Safety first
To avoid accidents, always use your crossbow outdoors. Never point it at anyone.

12 Cannons

To make large objects fly through the air we need a force large enough to overcome the pull of gravity. Centuries ago, people found that exploding gunpowder in a cannon provided the force to lift a cannonball into the air and push it forwards. However, once a cannonball has been expelled, gravity and air resistance slow the ball down, causing it to fall to the ground.

You will need
glue
thin card
a protractor
drawing pins
a long elastic band
thin wooden dowel
thick wooden dowel
tape and carpet tape
corrugated cardboard
a terracotta flowerpot
two cardboard tubes of different widths
ping pong ball to fit inside the larger tube

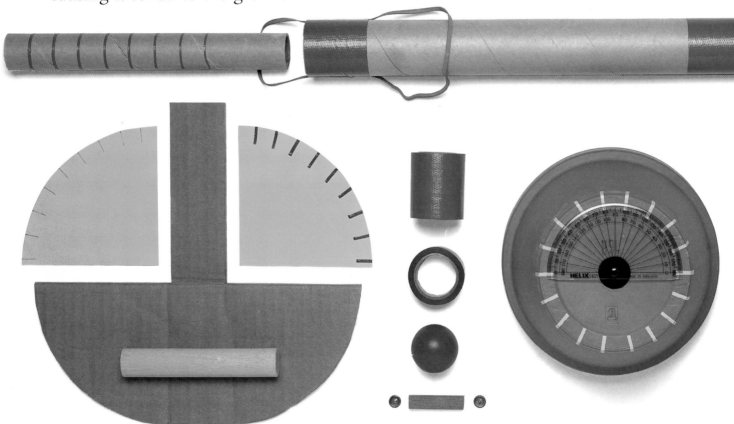

MAKE it WORK!

This home-made cannon uses the force from a stretched elastic band to fire cannonballs. The ball is forced upwards and forwards through the air, travelling in a curved path called a **trajectory**. But gravity is always acting on the ball, pulling it downwards towards the earth. You can use your cannon to investigate trajectories of cannonballs.

1 To make the turret, cut the corrugated cardboard and thin card into the shapes shown above left. Using the protractor, mark the card pieces with strips of tape every 10°.

2 Fold up the cardboard to make the turret and glue the card to its sides, as shown right. Join the sides of the turret at the top using a small piece of dowel and drawing pins.

3 Cut a length of thick dowel long enough to stand slightly higher than the flowerpot. Turn the flowerpot upside down and put the dowel through the hole.

4 Using the protractor, mark around the top of the flowerpot every 20°. Stick strips of brightly coloured tape over the marks as shown below. Glue the base of the turret to the thick dowel.

5 Take the narrow cardboard tube and mark every 3 cm along the outside. Place it inside the wider tube (the barrel of the cannon).

6 Using carpet tape, attach the elastic band to the bottom end of the barrel and to the bottom end of the narrow tube as shown.

7 Glue the barrel of the cannon to the movable flap inside the turret.

8 To fire the cannon, place the ball inside the barrel. Pull back the narrow, inner tube to stretch the elastic band, then release it.

Aim the barrel high and then low, pointing the turret in different directions. What happens when you pull the inside tube back a little way, or a long way? How do you make the ball travel further, or higher? By making a note of the measurements, you should be able to calculate where the ball will land.

Safety first!
When you are using your cannon, do not fire it indoors, and always aim it away from people.

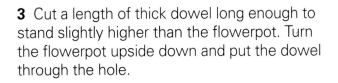

turret

barrel

*The first cannons, made in China as long ago as the 13th century, fired arrows. Later cannons fired stone or iron balls. One famous cannon, Mons Meg, built in 1453, fired cannonballs with **masses** of up to 180 kg.*

14 Kites

Kites were invented in China nearly 3,000 years ago. They fly because they get lift from the wind. The stronger the wind, the greater the force pushing the kite into the air. To keep flying, the kite must be held at an angle against the wind (called the angle of attack), just as a sail must face into the wind to move a yacht. Control lines are used to keep the kite at the correct angle to the wind.

1 Cut the nylon or polythene into a kite shape, 75 cm long and 70 cm across. Using a bradawl, make two holes in the kite, one 2 cm below the top point, the other 13 cm below. Make a hole about 2 cm in from each side point.

2 Being careful of your fingers, make two pairs of holes at right angles to each other through one plastic tube. Push the tube halfway into the hole at the top of the kite.

3 Pass the rigid dowel through the plastic tube, as in **a** below. Push the flexible dowel through the other holes in the tube, as in **b**.

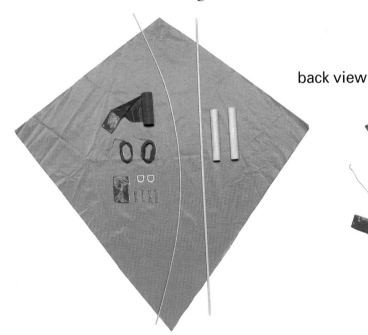

back view

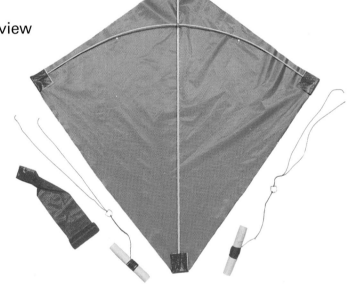

MAKE it WORK!
You can make your own kite and experiment with the forces that keep it in the air. Use the lines to control the kite and see how long you can keep it flying!

You will need
a bradawl	two metal rings
nylon cord	a craft knife
a long ribbon	carpet tape
five short plastic tubes	scissors

a 1 m square of polythene or nylon
thick, rigid dowel about 75 cm long
thin, flexible dowel about 85 cm long
two lengths of broom handle about 15 cm long

4 Make holes in four tubes. Push three tubes into holes at the sides and top of the kite. Stick the rigid dowel into the top and bottom tubes, and the flexible dowel into the side tubes. Fold the corners over the tubes and tape securely.

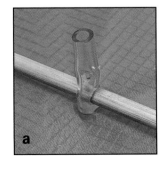
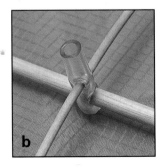

To make your kite fly, stand with your back to the wind. Then run backwards, pulling the kite to get it airborne.

To make the kite turn to the right, pull on the right handle. To make it fly straight again, pull on the left handle.

To make the kite turn to the left, pull on the left handle. To straighten the kite out, pull with your right hand.

front view

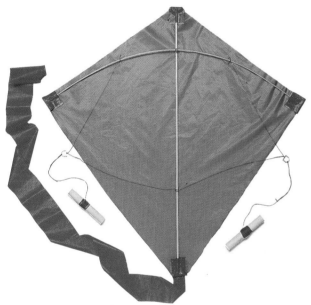

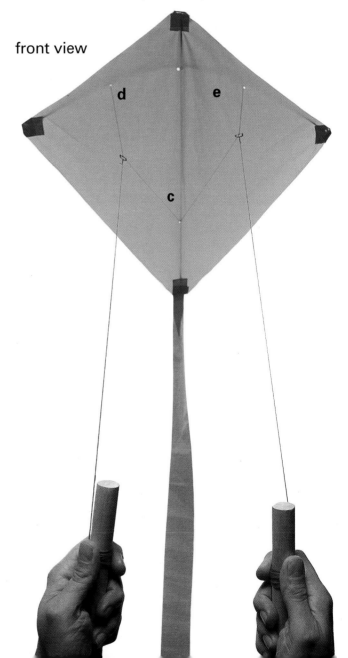

5 Make three holes as marked **c** to **e** (right). Take 80 cm of cord and tie the centre around the rigid dowel. Thread the loose ends through hole **c**. Turn the kite on to its front. Thread each end through a metal ring and through holes **d** and **e**, so that the metal rings stay on the front. Tie the ends to the flexible dowel as above.

6 Cut 20 m of cord in half. Tape one end of each half to a broom handle and tie the other to the rings. Wind the cord around the handles. Tape the tail ribbon on to the kite as shown.

About 1,000 years ago, the Chinese used kites to lift soldiers into the sky to survey battlefields.

16 Resisting Air

The force of air resistance acts on anything moving through the air. Without air resistance, or drag, objects would fall even faster than they do. The larger the object, the greater its air resistance. Parachutes use a large canopy to increase air resistance. This gives a slow fall and a soft landing.

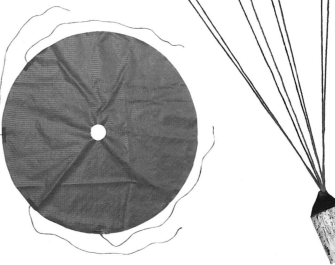

MAKE it WORK!

Can you find the best parachute design? Also, make a simple spinner and watch its wings spin as air resistance pushes against them.

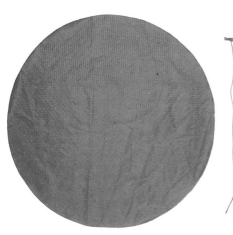

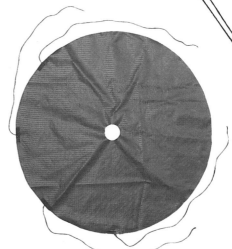

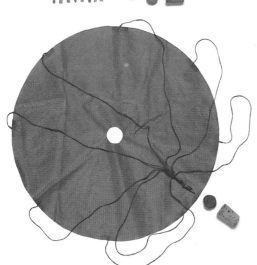

To make a parachute you will need

Plasticine	tape	scissors
tissue paper	a cork	
sewing thread	a small nail	

1 Cut out a circle with a 15 cm radius from the tissue paper to make the canopy. Make a hole in the centre.

2 Cut eight 30 cm pieces of sewing thread. Tape them at equal distances around the canopy edge, as shown above.

3 Tape the other ends of the threads to the nail and push the nail into the cork. Use Plasticine to secure the nail.

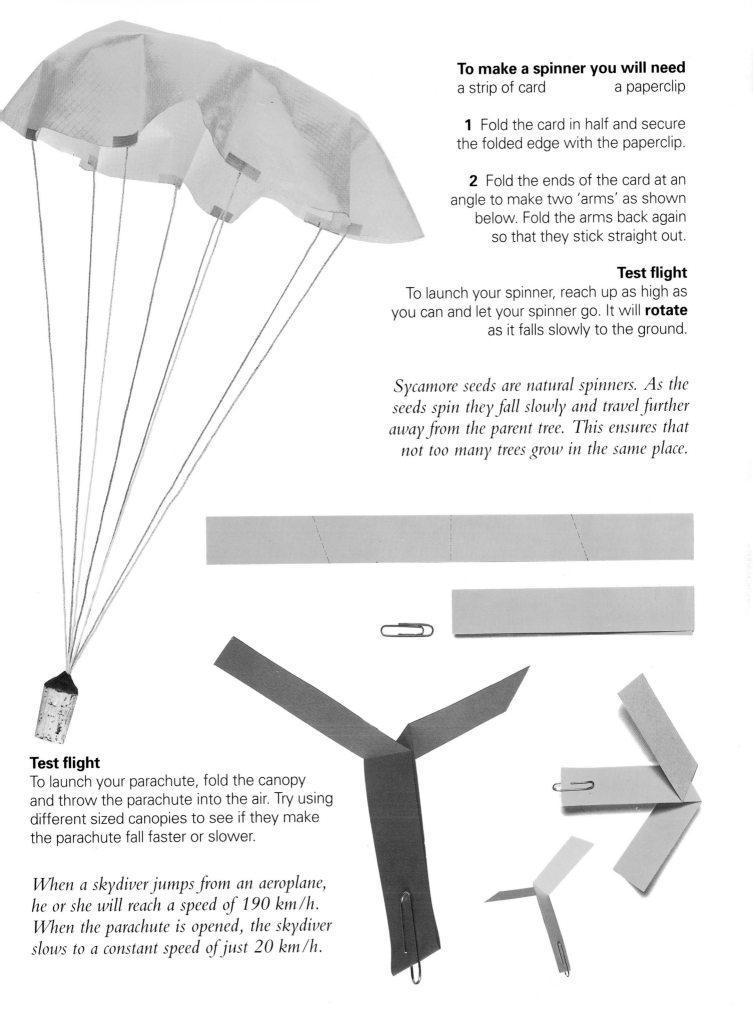

To make a spinner you will need

a strip of card   a paperclip

1 Fold the card in half and secure the folded edge with the paperclip.

2 Fold the ends of the card at an angle to make two 'arms' as shown below. Fold the arms back again so that they stick straight out.

Test flight

To launch your spinner, reach up as high as you can and let your spinner go. It will **rotate** as it falls slowly to the ground.

Sycamore seeds are natural spinners. As the seeds spin they fall slowly and travel further away from the parent tree. This ensures that not too many trees grow in the same place.

Test flight

To launch your parachute, fold the canopy and throw the parachute into the air. Try using different sized canopies to see if they make the parachute fall faster or slower.

When a skydiver jumps from an aeroplane, he or she will reach a speed of 190 km/h. When the parachute is opened, the skydiver slows to a constant speed of just 20 km/h.

Hot air is less **dense** than cold air. Hot air therefore rises through cold air and floats on it, just as oil floats on water. A balloon filled with hot air is less dense than cold air, so the whole balloon rises. Hot air can lift quite large balloons to great heights.

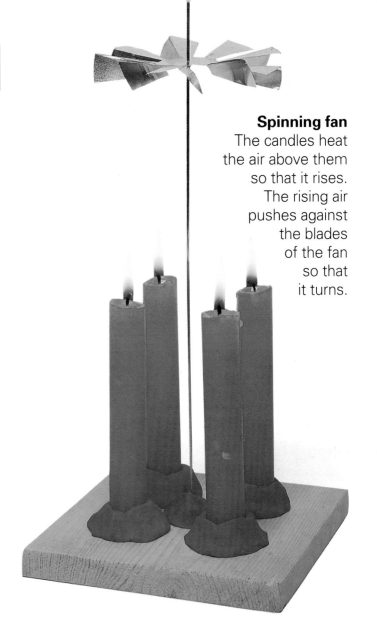

Spinning fan
The candles heat the air above them so that it rises. The rising air pushes against the blades of the fan so that it turns.

MAKE it WORK!
These experiments prove that hot air rises.
Be careful! Never leave lit candles unattended.

For the spinning fan you will need
four candles	stiff wire
a wooden block	Plasticine
an aluminium pie dish	a small bead

1 Fix the candles and the wire on to the wooden block with Plasticine, as shown. Tape the bead to the wire 15 cm above the candles.

2 Cut blades from the dish and angle them, as shown. Push the fan on to the wire so that it sits on the bead. Ask an adult to light the candles.

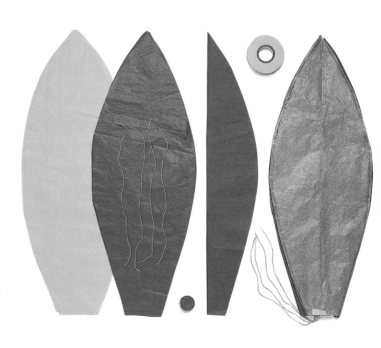

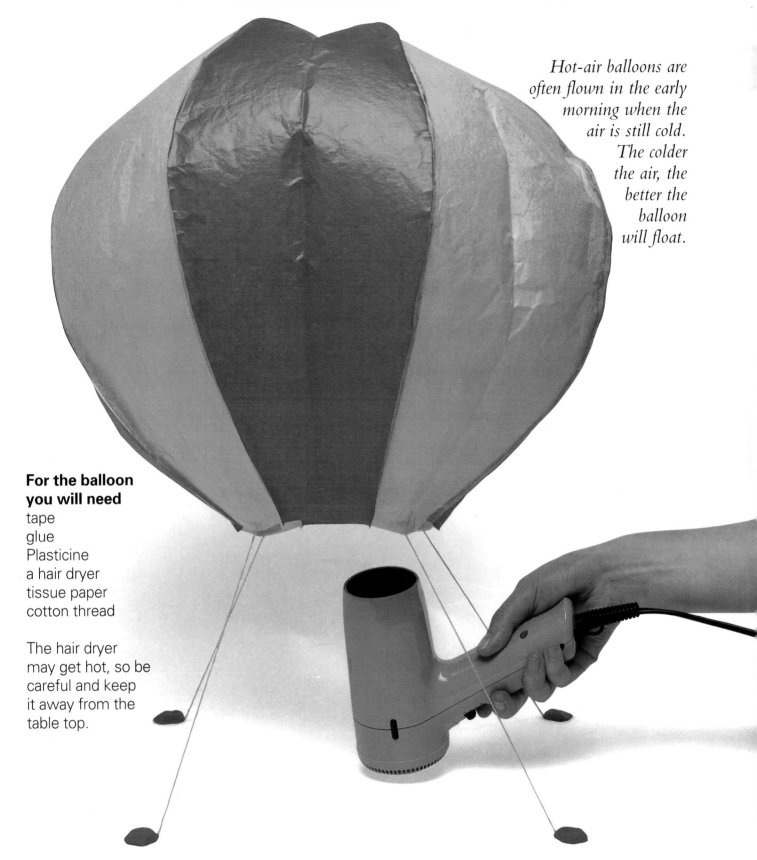

Hot-air balloons are often flown in the early morning when the air is still cold. The colder the air, the better the balloon will float.

For the balloon you will need
tape
glue
Plasticine
a hair dryer
tissue paper
cotton thread

The hair dryer may get hot, so be careful and keep it away from the table top.

1 Cut eight leaf-shaped sections of tissue paper, as shown left. Fold them in half and glue the edges together to make the balloon. Tape four threads to the bottom of the balloon. Fix the loose ends to a table with Plasticine.

2 Set the hair dryer to a low speed if you can. Point the nozzle upwards into the hole in the base of the balloon and turn the power on. The balloon will fill with hot air and will pull the threads tight, as shown above.

Airships are filled with a gas called helium. Helium floats in air because, like hot air, it is lighter than cold air. Helium gives enough lift to an airship to allow it to carry many passengers or cargo. Large propellers, driven by an engine, provide the thrust which pushes an airship forwards through the air. A tail fin gives the airship stability when it is in flight.

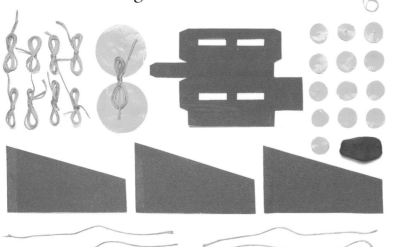

MAKE it WORK!

You can make an airship with helium-filled party balloons. You must tether your airship to the ground to stop it floating away.

You will need

tape	glue
scissors	string
thin card	Plasticine
four helium-filled balloons	

1 Cut out the tail fin, tailplane and cabin from the card, as shown above.

2 Cut eight pieces of string into equal lengths. Weight each string with a piece of Plasticine and tape to either side of the balloons to balance your airship, as shown above right.

3 Make your airship by gluing the balloons together. Tether it to the ground with string.

4 Cut a 18 cm long piece of thin card and fold it into a cabin shape, as above. Hang the cabin from the middle balloons with tape and string.

In the 1930s, airships used hydrogen gas instead of helium. Hydrogen is cheaper to produce than helium, but it can catch fire. The Hindenburg was a famous hydrogen-powered airship. It blew up in 1937, heralding the end of airship travel.

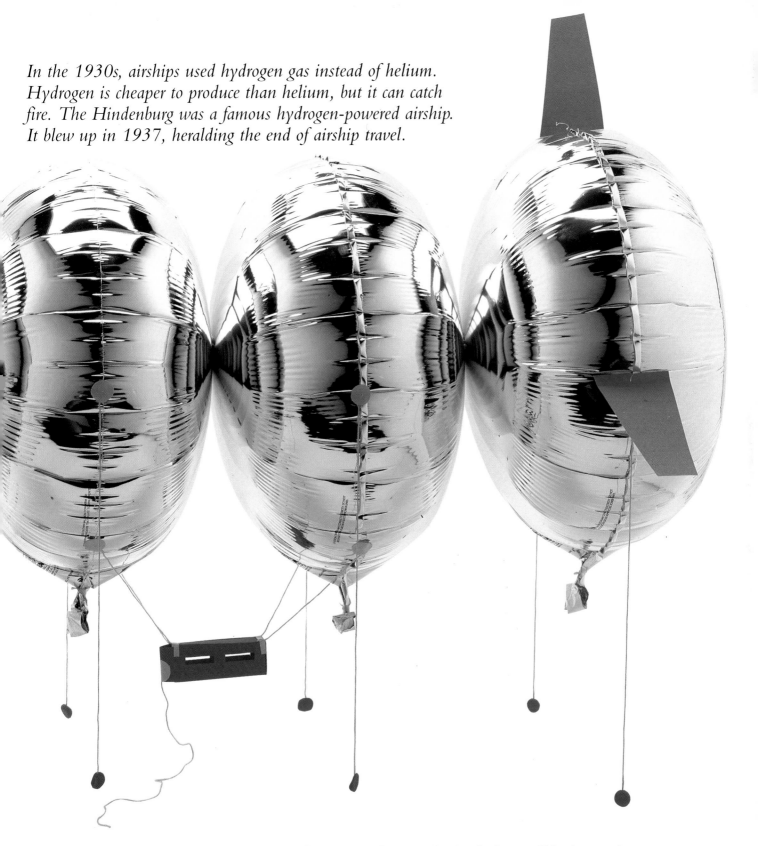

5 Attach the tail fin and tailplane pieces of card to the tail of your airship with glue, as shown.

6 Add or take away Plasticine from the ends of the strings hanging from each balloon until your airship hangs upright in the air.

Eventually, the helium will leak out of your airship. If it begins to come down, remove some Plasticine from the strings to make it lighter. Real airships contain bags called ballonets inside the helium. To bring the airship down, the ballonets are filled with air, which is heavier than helium.

Gliders have no source of **power**. As soon as they are launched they begin to fall back towards the ground. To keep flying, a glider pilot must find rising currents of warm air, called thermals, which lift the glider. When flying, the pilot controls the glider using pedals connected to the rudder.

1 Cut a 40 cm length of dowelling for the fuselage and a 10 cm length for the launcher.

2 To make the wings, cut out a piece of card 30 cm x 6 cm. Cut out a tailplane 20 cm x 6 cm at the widest point. Cut a tail fin 7.5 cm high and a rudder 7 cm high.

3 Glue a 6 cm strip of balsa wood to the centre of the wings. Glue the strip to the fuselage, so the wings are about 10 cm from the nose.

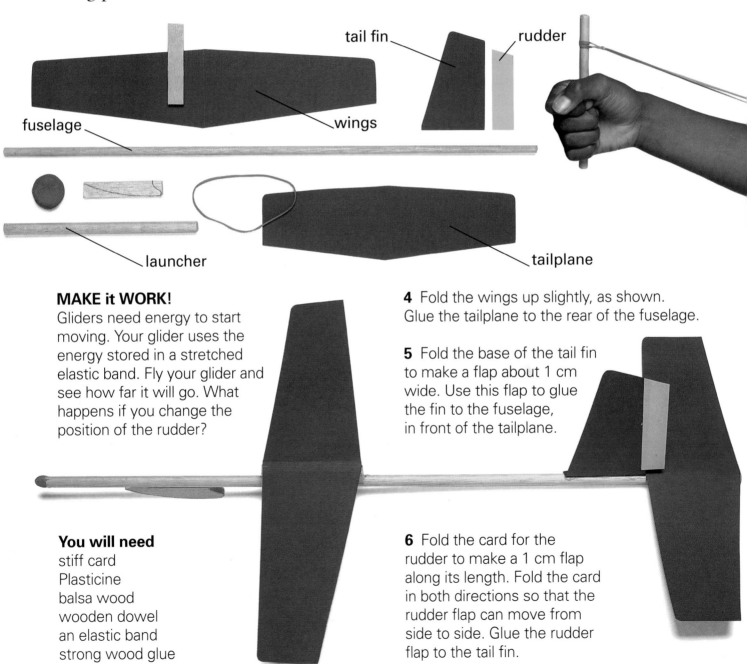

tail fin

rudder

fuselage

wings

launcher

tailplane

MAKE it WORK!
Gliders need energy to start moving. Your glider uses the energy stored in a stretched elastic band. Fly your glider and see how far it will go. What happens if you change the position of the rudder?

4 Fold the wings up slightly, as shown. Glue the tailplane to the rear of the fuselage.

5 Fold the base of the tail fin to make a flap about 1 cm wide. Use this flap to glue the fin to the fuselage, in front of the tailplane.

You will need
stiff card
Plasticine
balsa wood
wooden dowel
an elastic band
strong wood glue

6 Fold the card for the rudder to make a 1 cm flap along its length. Fold the card in both directions so that the rudder flap can move from side to side. Glue the rudder flap to the tail fin.

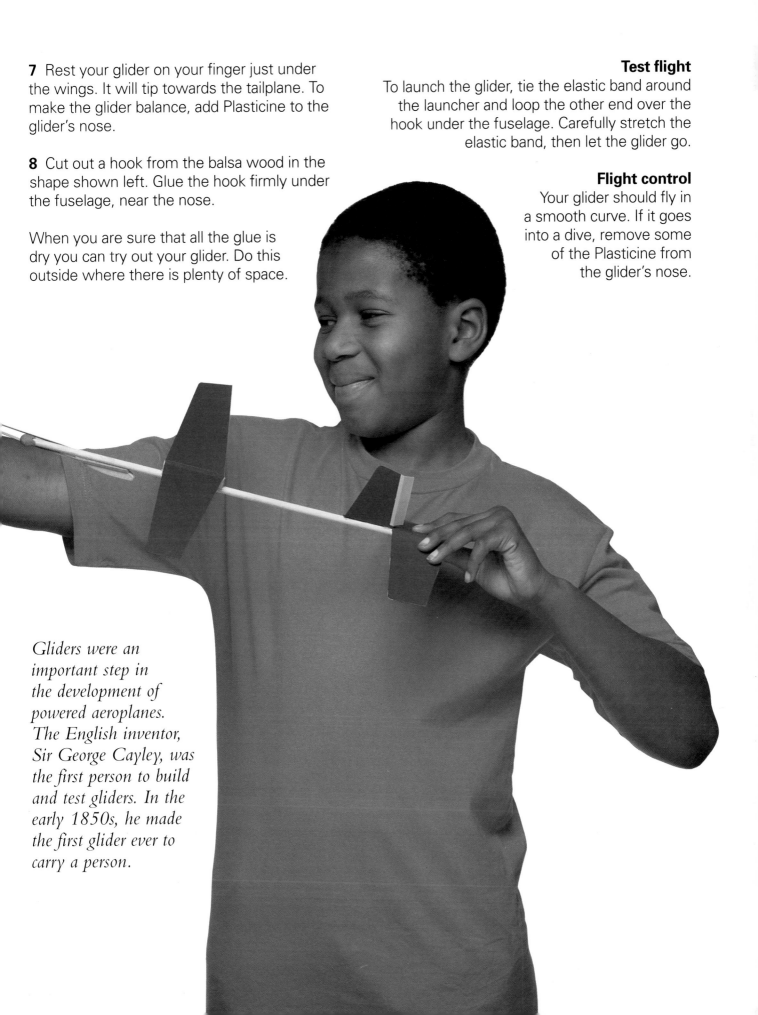

7 Rest your glider on your finger just under the wings. It will tip towards the tailplane. To make the glider balance, add Plasticine to the glider's nose.

8 Cut out a hook from the balsa wood in the shape shown left. Glue the hook firmly under the fuselage, near the nose.

When you are sure that all the glue is dry you can try out your glider. Do this outside where there is plenty of space.

Test flight
To launch the glider, tie the elastic band around the launcher and loop the other end over the hook under the fuselage. Carefully stretch the elastic band, then let the glider go.

Flight control
Your glider should fly in a smooth curve. If it goes into a dive, remove some of the Plasticine from the glider's nose.

Gliders were an important step in the development of powered aeroplanes. The English inventor, Sir George Cayley, was the first person to build and test gliders. In the early 1850s, he made the first glider ever to carry a person.

Imagine cutting the wings off an aeroplane. Looking at the cut end, you would find that the top surface of the wing is curved, while the bottom surface is flatter. Most wings have this shape, called an aerofoil. Air moves around the aerofoil as the aeroplane flies. This provides the lift which keeps the aeroplane in the air.

You will need

a protractor
cotton thread
a drill or bradawl
a wooden block
a desk fan
stiff wire
scissors
a bead
card
glue
tape

MAKE it WORK!

Using a fan to make air flow past an aerofoil, you can investigate the force that keeps an aeroplane in the air. How does the aerofoil perform when it is set at different angles? To be safe, use a fan with a cage or rubber blades, like the one shown here.

1 Cut a rectangle of card measuring 10 cm x 30 cm. Draw two lines across the card, 1 cm from one edge and 1.5 cm from the other.

2 Fold the card in half. Fold the 1 cm wide edge of the card so that it fits flat against the 1.5 cm line at the other end. You should have a shape with a curved top, as shown right. This is an aerofoil.

3 Lie the aerofoil on its flat surface. Ask an adult to help make two holes through the centre of the aerofoil's widest part, one directly above the other.

4 Push the bead on to one end of the wire, bending the wire to hold the bead in place. Push the rest of the wire through the holes in the aerofoil.

5 Make a hole in the middle of the wooden block, just big enough to hold the end of the wire. Push the wire into the block so that it stands firmly in the wood. You should be able to change the angle of the wire.

6 Attach the protractor to one side of the block, as shown below, using tape.

7 To help you see how air moves over the wing, attach pieces of cotton thread to the aerofoil. The threads will follow the flow of air.

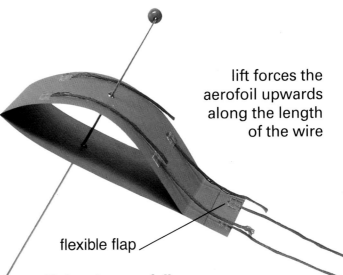

lift forces the aerofoil upwards along the length of the wire

flexible flap

protractor measures the angle of the aerofoil to the airflow

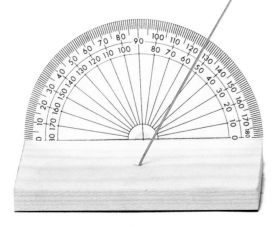

Flying the aerofoil

Stand the fan in front of the aerofoil, making sure that the rounded edge is facing the fan. This edge is the leading edge and the other is the trailing edge. The curve of the aerofoil means that air moving over the wing travels faster than air moving below the wing.

Fast-moving air does not press against objects as much as slow-moving air. Therefore there is less pressure on the top of the wing than there is on the underside. The higher pressure on the underside pushes up and lifts the wing. The amount of lift generated by pressure depends on the angle of the wing to the airflow.

*Over two hundred years ago Daniel Bernouilli was the first person to realize that air exerts less **pressure** the faster it moves. Today, this fact is known as the Bernouilli effect.*

When the aerofoil is turned upside down, the air forces it to the ground. To produce an upward force, the curved side of the wing must be on top.

The aerofoil creates good lift with its flat edge at a small angle to the stream of air. It is pushed up the wire by the lift force.

The size of the lift force increases with the angle of the aerofoil to the wind. Here the aerofoil travels quickly to the very end of the wire and stays there.

Most early aeroplanes were triplanes (three sets of wings), or biplanes (two sets). Several short sets of wings gave the aeroplanes the lift they needed to fly. A monoplane, with just one set of wings, needs longer wings to produce the same amount of lift, but creates less drag than biplanes or triplanes. Most modern aeroplanes are monoplanes.

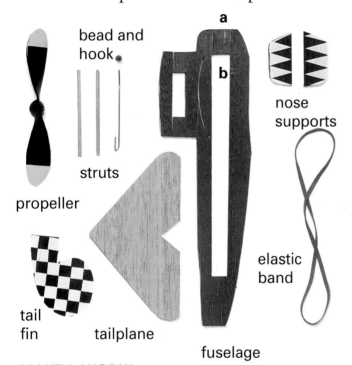

bead and hook

struts

propeller

tail fin

tailplane

fuselage

a

b

nose supports

elastic band

MAKE it WORK!
You can make a triplane using balsa wood. You will need to use **struts** to keep the wings rigid.

You will need
glue
a cork
a stapler
stiff wire
a hand drill
a paperclip
a small bead
model propeller
thin balsa wood
a long elastic band

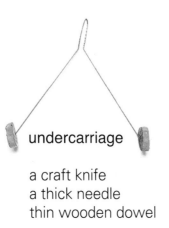

undercarriage

a craft knife
a thick needle
thin wooden dowel

1 Cut the wing pieces from the balsa wood as shown below. Make two small holes, one in each end of the middle wing, for the struts.

2 Cut balsa wood shapes for the fuselage, tail fin and tailplane. Then decorate the pieces, as shown.

3 Glue the tailplane and tail fin to the back of the fuselage, as shown right.

4 Use a thick needle to make a hole in the nose of the fuselage, from **a** to **b** (as shown left). This is the propeller shaft. Cut out two identical nose supports and glue to either side of the fuselage for extra strength. Allow the glue to dry.

5 Straighten the paperclip out and bend one end to form a hook. Push the straight end through the propeller shaft so that the hooked end points backwards, towards the tailplane.

6 Push the bead and then the propeller over the wire poking out of the front of the nose. Bend the end of the wire over to hold the bead and propeller in place. The bead forms a bearing which allows the propeller to spin around freely.

three sets of wings

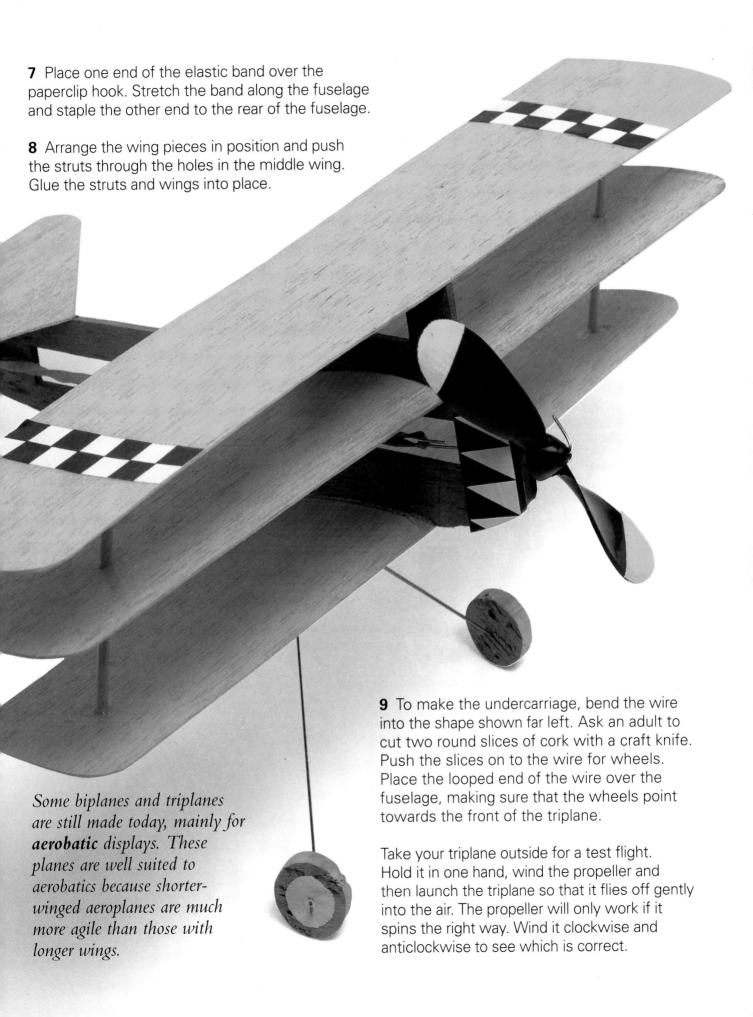

7 Place one end of the elastic band over the paperclip hook. Stretch the band along the fuselage and staple the other end to the rear of the fuselage.

8 Arrange the wing pieces in position and push the struts through the holes in the middle wing. Glue the struts and wings into place.

*Some biplanes and triplanes are still made today, mainly for **aerobatic** displays. These planes are well suited to aerobatics because shorter-winged aeroplanes are much more agile than those with longer wings.*

9 To make the undercarriage, bend the wire into the shape shown far left. Ask an adult to cut two round slices of cork with a craft knife. Push the slices on to the wire for wheels. Place the looped end of the wire over the fuselage, making sure that the wheels point towards the front of the triplane.

Take your triplane outside for a test flight. Hold it in one hand, wind the propeller and then launch the triplane so that it flies off gently into the air. The propeller will only work if it spins the right way. Wind it clockwise and anticlockwise to see which is correct.

28 Delta Wings

Supersonic aeroplanes can travel faster than the speed of sound. They look different from other modern aircraft, often having triangular wings called delta wings. Aircraft with delta wings perform very well at high speeds. Delta wings help to reduce the **sonic boom** that is heard on the ground as an aeroplane travels faster than sound.

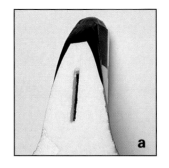

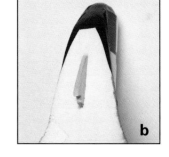

a

b

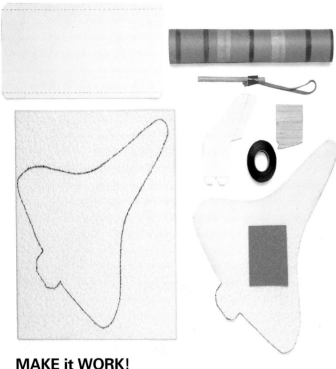

MAKE it WORK!
The space shuttle is a reusable aircraft built by **NASA** in the United States. It is well-suited to travelling fast through the Earth's atmosphere because it has delta wings. You can make your own model of the shuttle.

You will need
glue
thin card
sandpaper
balsa wood
a craft knife
masking tape

wooden dowel
a ping pong ball
a polystyrene tile
a large elastic band
three cardboard tubes

1 Tape the cardboard tubes together, end to end, to form the fuselage of your shuttle. Glue the ball inside one end of the fuselage so that one half of it is visible.

2 Copy the delta wing shape on to the polystyrene tile – the wings should be the same length as the shuttle fuselage. Ask an adult to help you cut it out. Smooth the edges of the wings with the sandpaper.

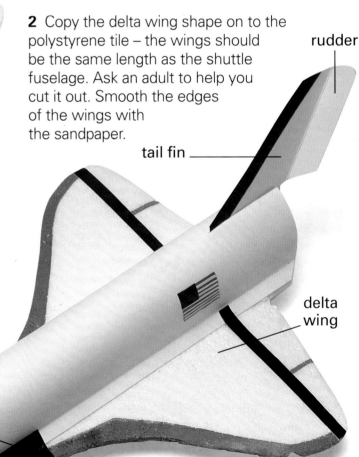

rudder

tail fin

delta wing

launcher

fuselage

3 Cut out the tail fin shape from the card, as shown left. Score and fold along the dotted lines on the base of the fin and the rudder.

4 Cut a rectangle of card the same length as the fuselage and wide enough to wrap two-thirds of the way around it. Score along the dotted lines, as shown left, then glue the card over the fuselage.

5 Make a 4 cm slit through the fuselage and card at the tail end of the plane. Slot the tail fin gently into it. Glue the flaps at the base of the tail fin inside the cardboard tube fuselage.

6 Place the fuselage in the centre of the wings. Tape the cardboard flaps of the fuselage to the wings on both sides.

7 Cut out the shape of the launching hook from balsa wood, as shown left.

8 Carefully cut a slit in the underside of the fuselage, a short distance from the nose, as shown in **a** above left. Glue the hook as in **b**.

9 Cut a length of wooden dowel and tie the elastic band to one end to form the launcher, as shown left. Decorate your model with tape so that it looks like a space shuttle.

The space shuttle has a mass of 97.5 tonnes, is 37 m long (its fuel tank is 47 m) and must travel at 11.2 km/second to get into orbit. It is designed for at least 100 space flights.

Test flight

Use the launcher to fly your space shuttle. Loop the elastic band over the hook under the nose. Hold the launcher in one hand and the shuttle firmly in the other. Stretch the elastic band and tilt the shuttle upwards slightly, then release it. Always launch your shuttle outside and away from other people. For an alternative shuttle launch, see pages 44 to 45.

The first space shuttle was launched on April 12, 1981 in the United States.

Aeroplanes with triangular, swept-back wings, or delta wings, are well-suited to high-speed flight. But at low speeds they do not produce as much lift as a plane with ordinary wings. A swing-wing aeroplane has wings which change during flight between delta wings and ordinary wings, according to its speed.

2 Make the fuselage sides by cutting out two identical card shapes, as shown below. Score and fold the card along the dotted lines. Punch a hole in each side as shown.

3 Cut out two identical wing shapes and punch a hole in each as shown. Decorate the wing tips with strips of coloured tape.

4 Attach the wings to the fuselage by pushing the fasteners through both holes and folding the ends out flat underneath.

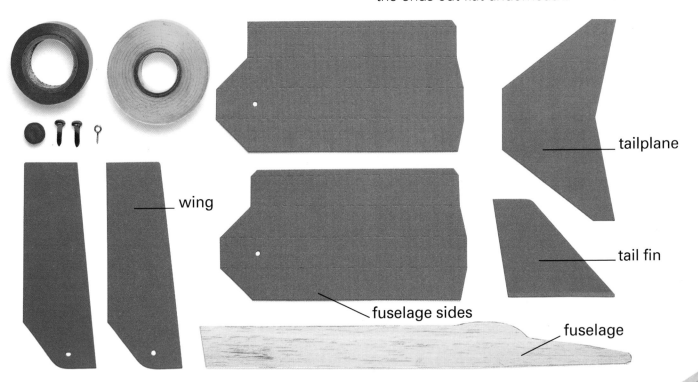

wing

tailplane

tail fin

fuselage sides

fuselage

MAKE it WORK!
If you make a swing-wing glider, you can swing the wings of the glider between two positions and find out how this effects the glider's flight.

You will need
glue	a craft knife
paint	a hole punch
thick card	coloured tape
Plasticine	two paper fasteners
balsa wood	the launcher from page 28
a small hook	

1 Ask an adult to help cut the fuselage. Paint it and stick on window shapes cut from the tape.

5 Fold both sides of the fuselage into a long box. Hold the boxes together by gluing the narrow flap inside. When the glue is dry attach them to either side of the balsa wood fuselage, also using glue. The angled end should face towards the nose.

6 Cut out the tailplane and tail fin and decorate them with coloured tape. Score and fold a narrow flap at the bottom of the tail fin. Glue the flap to the rear of the fuselage and fold the tail fin so that it stands up straight.

7 Cut the tailplane in half to make two smaller wings. Glue each half to the top of the fuselage, at the base of the tail fin.

8 Screw the hook into the underside of the glider, about halfway along the nose.

9 Support the model glider with your finger just under the wings. In order to fly properly, your model must be perfectly balanced. To do this add or remove small pieces of Plasticine to the nose.

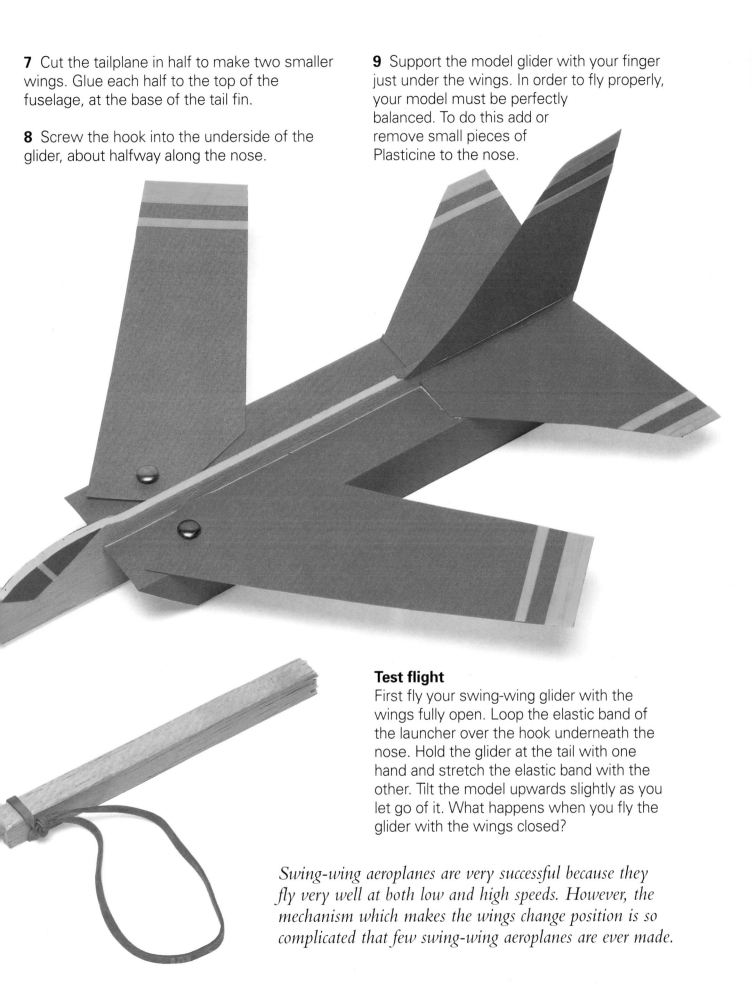

Test flight
First fly your swing-wing glider with the wings fully open. Loop the elastic band of the launcher over the hook underneath the nose. Hold the glider at the tail with one hand and stretch the elastic band with the other. Tilt the model upwards slightly as you let go of it. What happens when you fly the glider with the wings closed?

Swing-wing aeroplanes are very successful because they fly very well at both low and high speeds. However, the mechanism which makes the wings change position is so complicated that few swing-wing aeroplanes are ever made.

An aeroplane propeller provides thrust in two ways. It has curved blades which disturb the air as they rotate. This creates high-pressure air behind the propeller, which pushes the propeller and the aeroplane forwards. At the same time, the spinning propeller pushes air backwards. This also pushes the plane forwards. A propeller needs a source of power, usually an engine.

Propellers are curved like an aeroplane's wing. They produce a force in the same way that a wing produces lift, but this push is directed forwards, rather than upwards.

MAKE it WORK!
By making a model propeller you will see how the air is pushed backwards as it turns. Your propeller does not need an engine. You will provide the energy to keep it turning.

You will need
a cork	glue
thin card	string
Plasticine	ribbons
two straws	hand drill
thick balsa wood	a craft knife
thick and thin wooden dowel	

1 Ask an adult to cut two rectangles, 5 cm x 2 cm, from the balsa wood, with a craft knife.

2 Now ask the adult to drill a hole in the centre of each piece, large enough for the thick wooden dowel to pass through.

3 Cut two more blocks, 10 cm x 2 cm, from the wood. Glue the blocks together, with the holes facing each other, to form a frame as shown below.

4 Ask an adult to drill a hole through the top of the cork.

5 Now make a second hole in the other end of the cork, going halfway up into the middle.

6 Push a 30 cm length of thin dowel right through the hole going across the top of the cork. Push the end of a 15 cm length of thick dowel up into the centre of the cork.

7 For the propeller blades, first cut four rectangles, 12 cm x 6 cm, from card.

8 Draw a line down the centre of two of the rectangles and glue a straw along each line. Glue the other card rectangles on top.

9 Slide the straws on to the thin dowelling and secure the ends with Plasticine. Position the blades so that they are at angles to each other.

10 Push the long end of the thick dowel through both holes in the wooden frame.

To see your propeller at work, hold the frame in one hand and twist the thick dowel with the other. Suspend ribbons on a string and point your propeller at them. Which way do you turn the dowel in order to make the ribbons flutter? What happens to the ribbons when you turn the propeller in the other direction?

In 1979, a propeller-driven aeroplane, the Gossamer Albatross, flew 35 km between England and France. This plane was unusual because it had pedals and a chain, like those on a bicycle, to transmit power to the propeller.

An aeroplane with a propeller needs a source of power to make the propeller turn. People have used pedals and even electric motors driven by solar power to turn propellers. Today, most aircraft have propellers driven by internal combustion engines, which are very powerful, yet light. These engines produce power by burning **fuel**.

You will need

a cork	a stapler
stiff wire	Plasticine
strong glue	balsa wood
a paperclip	a craft knife
a model propeller	a small bead
a long elastic band	insulating tape
a hand drill or bradawl	

1 Ask an adult to help you cut out a 1 cm x 25 cm strip of balsa wood for the fuselage. Then cut a 2.5 cm wide rectangle for the nose.

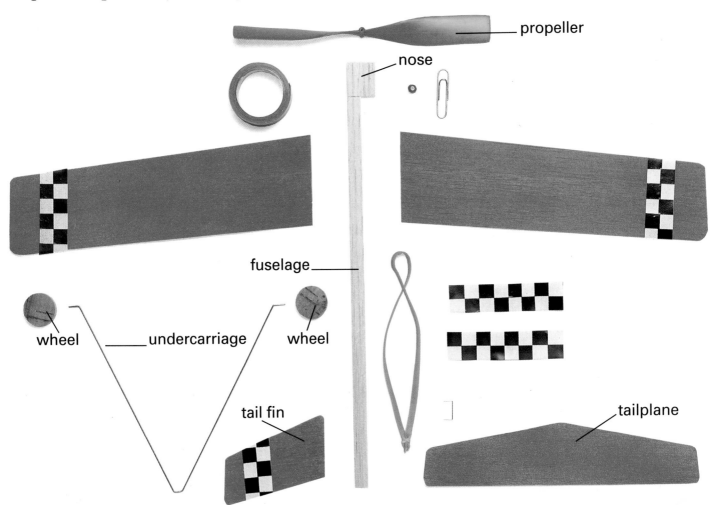

propeller

nose

wheel   undercarriage   wheel

fuselage

tail fin

tailplane

MAKE it WORK!

An elastic band drives the propeller on this model plane. Twisting the elastic band stores energy in it. When the model is released, this energy untwists the elastic band and turns the propeller. The tighter you twist the elastic band, the faster the propeller turns.

2 Glue the nose to one end of the fuselage, then wrap insulating tape around it. Make a small hole through the length of the nose, beneath the fuselage, with the drill or bradawl.

3 Staple the elastic band to the underside of the fuselage, about 5 cm from the tail end.

4 Straighten out the paperclip and push it through the hole in the nose. Slide the bead and the propeller on to the paperclip. Bend the end of the paperclip to hold them in place. Bend the other end of the paperclip on the underside of the fuselage and hook the elastic band over it.

5 Ask an adult to make two 4 cm slits in the tail-end of the fuselage with a craft knife. Make one slit along the top and the other through the side of the tail as shown below.

6 Cut a 5 cm x 7 cm tail fin from the balsa wood and a 18 cm x 4 cm tailplane. Slot both pieces into the fuselage, as shown below.

7 Cut two 20 cm x 6 cm wings and glue them to the top of the fuselage so that they are slightly angled upwards. Bend the wire into the shape of the undercarriage. Cut two slices off the cork and stick them on to the end of the wire to make the wheels. Now position the undercarriage over the fuselage.

To fly your plane, hold it gently behind the wings and wind up the propeller. Push the model into the air and release the propeller.

The first successful propelled flight of an aeroplane was in 1871. The propeller was powered by a wound-up elastic band and the aeroplane was only 50 cm long.

Flight control
If your aeroplane is not stable, wind the propeller in the other direction. The plane should fly in a gentle curve. If it dives, add some Plasticine to the tail. If it stalls, or loses lift, add a little to the nose.

A pilot controls an aircraft in flight using levers and pedals in the cockpit to move the **control surfaces**. Most planes have three types of control surface – ailerons, elevators and the rudder – which allow the pilot to change direction in the air.

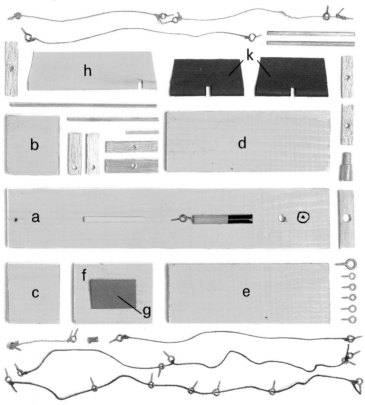

MAKE it WORK!

You can see how a pilot's controls work by making the model cockpit on the next few pages. Use the model glider on page 22 to see how the rudder can control flight.

You will need

saw	thin card
string	strong glue
a hand drill	a craft knife
a long tack	a large hook
balsa wood	a large eyelet hook
drinking straws	three rubber bungs
small eyelet hooks	thick and thin dowel
plastic tube to fit thick dowel	
a long plank of wood 1 cm thick x 8 cm wide	

The aeroplane base

1 Ask an adult to saw the plank into six pieces (**a** to **f**) to make the base shown below.

2 Drill a large hole in one end of the fuselage for the thick dowel (rudder pedal) and a smaller hole in the other end for the thin dowel (rudder).

3 Glue the base pieces together (apart from the tail fin) and glue the rubber bungs under the base for support.

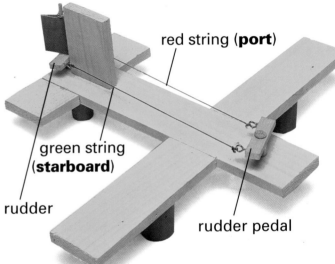

red string (**port**)

green string (**starboard**)

rudder

rudder pedal

The rudder: steering or turning

1 Ask an adult to cut two 7 cm x 2 cm bars of balsa wood. Drill a large hole in the centre of one (the rudder pedal) and a small hole in the centre of the other (the rudder). Screw one small eyelet hook into each end of both bars, as shown.

2 To make the rudder pedal, push 4 cm of thick dowel into the hole in the fuselage nose. Cover the dowel with 2 cm of tubing. Push a long tack through the pedal with the large hole and then into the dowel, keeping the eyelets facing the tail.

3 Make a rudder flap by gluing a piece of card 8 cm x 6 cm (**g**) around a 8 cm length of straw. To fix the flap to the rudder, cut 12 cm of thin dowel and push it through the straw. Push the dowel through the hole in the remaining balsa wood block, a 2 cm length of straw and, lastly, through the hole in the f uselage tail.

4 Screw a large eyelet hook into the back of the tail fin. Glue the tail fin into place, sliding the hook over the thin dowel holding the rudder flap. When the glue is dry, tie red and green string between the eyelets on the rudder and pedal.

The control stick

1 Cut 9 cm of thick dowel for the control stick. Screw one small eyelet into the bottom of the stick and another 3 cm from the base. Screw a hook into the fuselage, behind the rudder pedal. Slide the eyelet over the hook in the fuselage.

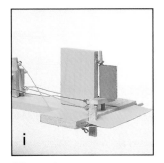

i

j

The elevator

1 Cut a balsa wood bar, 7 cm x 2 cm, and drill a small hole through the centre. Screw an eyelet into each end, on the same side, as **i** above.

2 Cut a 20 cm x 15 cm piece of card and fold it in half. Glue a straw along the inside fold. Cut a 3 cm slit near one end, as shown left in **h**.

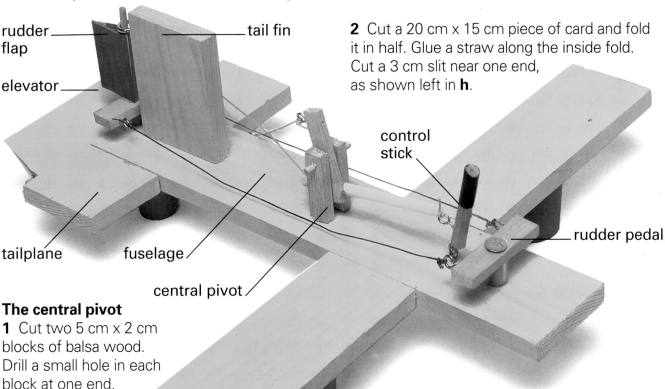

rudder flap — — tail fin

elevator —

control stick

tailplane   fuselage

central pivot

rudder pedal

wing

The central pivot

1 Cut two 5 cm x 2 cm blocks of balsa wood. Drill a small hole in each block at one end.

2 Cut another 7 cm x 2 cm block and drill a small hole through the centre. Screw an eyelet into each end on opposite sides as above. Tie a 25 cm piece of string to each eyelet.

3 Position the larger block between the smaller ones as above, so that the holes line up. Glue the outer blocks to the fuselage. When dry, slot in the middle block and push a length of thin dowel through all three holes.

3 Screw two eyelets to the back of the tailplane, 21 cm apart. Slot the bar vertically into the card flap. Slide a 22 cm thin dowel through the eyelets, elevator flap and bar, as in **j** above.

4 Tie a string from the top of the central pivot to the bottom of the bar; and another from the bottom of the pivot to the top of the bar. Then thread a 7 cm string through a piece of straw. Tie one end to the eyelet in the control stick, the other to the eyelet at the base of the pivot.

Now move the control stick and rudder pedal to see the effect on the elevator and rudder.

Aeroplanes have movable flaps called ailerons at the trailing edge of each wing. They are designed so that when one is up, the other is down. Ailerons are used with the rudder in a turning manoeuvre called **banking**.

MAKE it WORK!

By using the rudder pedal and control stick on pages 36-37, you can see how an aeroplane can turn, climb and dive. Now add ailerons to learn how more advanced manoeuvres, such as **yaw**, banking or rolling are carried out.

The ailerons: rolling or banking

Make the ailerons in the same way that you made the elevator and rudder (pages 36 to 37).

1 Cut two pieces of balsa wood 7 cm long x 2 cm wide. Drill a hole in the centre of both bars, wide enough for thin dowel to pass through.

2 Cut two card rectangles 14 cm x 10 cm. Fold them in half and glue a straw along the fold (see **k**, page 36). Glue the flaps around the straw.

3 Cut a notch 1 cm deep in the centre of each folded card (through the straw).

4 Screw two small hooks into the ends of each balsa wood bar. Then screw two hooks into the trailing edge of each wing 10.5 cm apart.

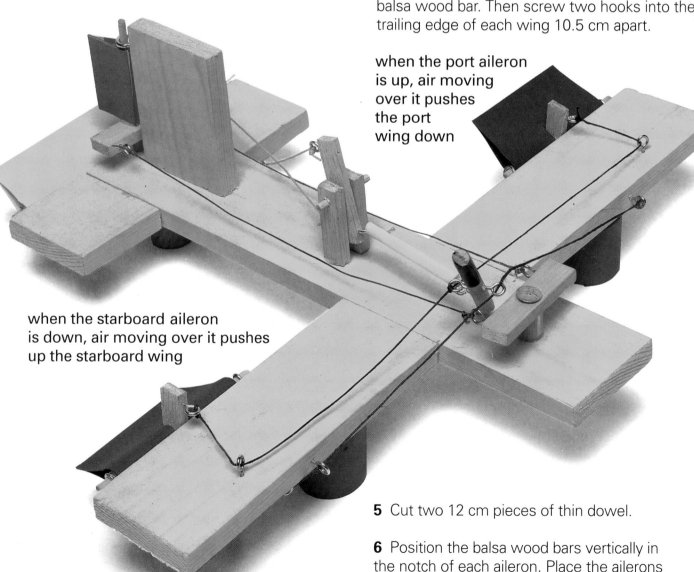

when the port aileron is up, air moving over it pushes the port wing down

when the starboard aileron is down, air moving over it pushes up the starboard wing

5 Cut two 12 cm pieces of thin dowel.

6 Position the balsa wood bars vertically in the notch of each aileron. Place the ailerons between the each pair of hooks on the wings.

 left turn

right turn

Left and right turning or banking

By adding ailerons to the glider you made on page 22, you can make it turn to the left and right, as above. Use blue card for making the ailerons, as below.

When the starboard aileron is up and the port aileron is down, the aeroplane rolls to the right. When the rudder is moved to the right at the same time, the aeroplane turns smoothly to the right. Reverse the positions to make a left turn.

Early aeroplanes did not have ailerons. Pilots changed direction in midair by pulling levers which made the whole wing change shape.

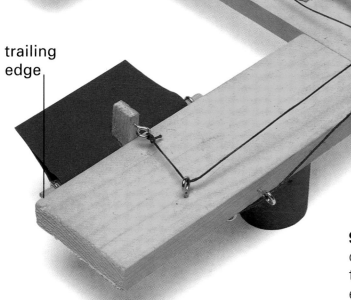

trailing edge

7 Slide the dowel through the hooks, aileron and balsa wood to hold in place.

8 Screw three small eyelets into each wing: one on top, the second under the wing, directly below the first, and the third in the centre of the front edge of the wing. Screw two more hooks on to either side of the control stick.

9 Tie 40 cm of string to both eyelets in the top of the aileron bars. Thread the string through the eyelets in the top of the wings and tie the ends to one eyelet in the control stick, as shown above. The string should be taut.

10 Repeat step 9, but thread the string from the bottom of the aileron bar, underneath the wings, to the other eyelet on the control stick.

Moving the control stick to the left and right pulls the strings and raises and lowers the two ailerons. When one is up the other is down.

The rotor of a helicopter acts like a cross between an aeroplane wing and a propeller. It provides both lift to keep the helicopter in the air and thrust to push it forwards. The helicopter can take off and land vertically, move in any direction, or remain hanging in one place in the air.

3 Draw a circle, with a diameter of 2 cm, in the centre. Cut along the solid lines to the circle and then score and fold along the dotted lines. Glue a circle of different coloured card inside the central circle on the top of your rotor.

4 Use a bradawl to make a small hole in the middle of a cork. Push a 12 cm length of dowel into the hole. Stick the rotor of your spinner on to the cork. Wind the string around the dowel and then push the dowel through the cotton reel as shown below.

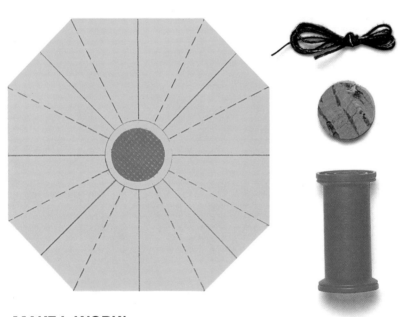

Holding the reel in one hand and the string in the other, pull the string and launch your spinner. If it fails, try winding the string the other way.

The design of the helicopter was based on a toy from 16th-century China.

MAKE it WORK!

You can make two models to look at the way a helicopter rotor works. Both will take off if you set them spinning fast enough.

To make a rotor you will need

a cork	glue
stiff card	string
a bradawl	a protractor
a cotton reel	thin wooden dowel

1 Cut the card into a 10 cm square. Draw two solid lines through the centre and two across the diagonal, as shown. Trim the corners.

2 Line up the centre of the protractor with the centre of the square and draw dotted lines at 20° to each side of the diagonal lines.

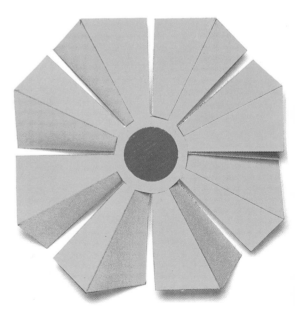

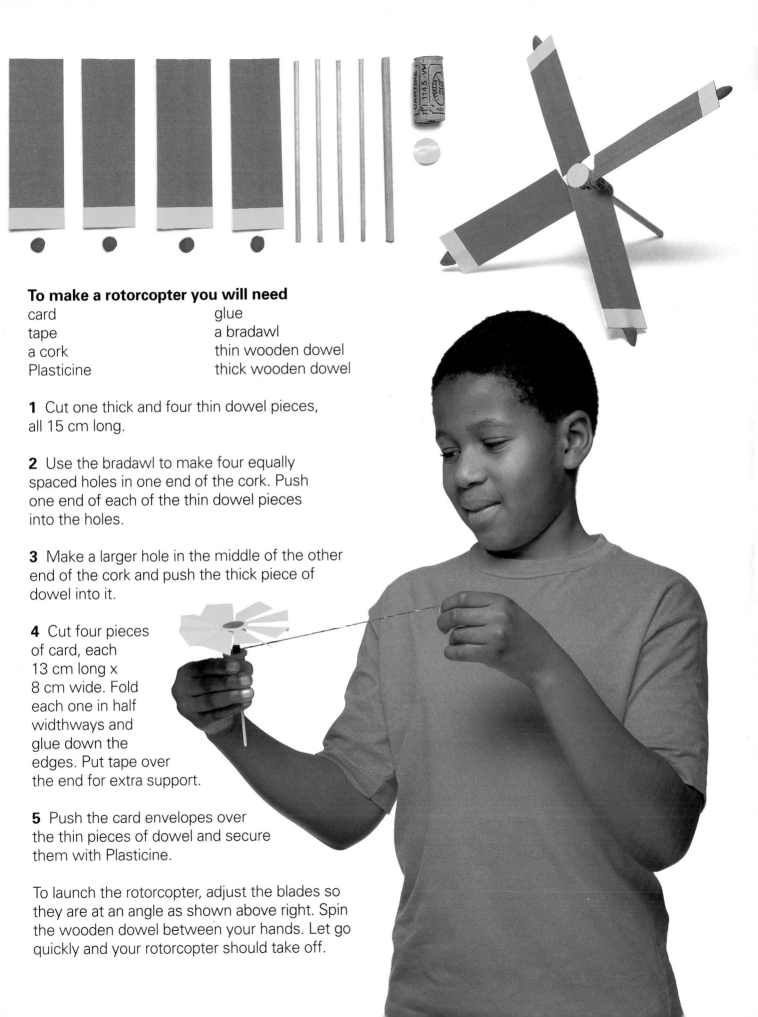

To make a rotorcopter you will need

card

tape

a cork

Plasticine

glue

a bradawl

thin wooden dowel

thick wooden dowel

1 Cut one thick and four thin dowel pieces, all 15 cm long.

2 Use the bradawl to make four equally spaced holes in one end of the cork. Push one end of each of the thin dowel pieces into the holes.

3 Make a larger hole in the middle of the other end of the cork and push the thick piece of dowel into it.

4 Cut four pieces of card, each 13 cm long x 8 cm wide. Fold each one in half widthways and glue down the edges. Put tape over the end for extra support.

5 Push the card envelopes over the thin pieces of dowel and secure them with Plasticine.

To launch the rotorcopter, adjust the blades so they are at an angle as shown above right. Spin the wooden dowel between your hands. Let go quickly and your rotorcopter should take off.

42 Jet Engines

A jet engine is much more powerful than a propeller. It works by burning fuel to heat up air which is taken in at the front of the engine. The air expands as it is heated and leaves at high speed from the back of the engine. The escaping gases produce a strong forward thrust, which pushes the aircraft through the air.

For the jet balloons you will need

tape	balloon pump
string	drinking straws
long balloons	

1 Thread a piece of straw on to the string. Tie the string to two chairs, placed quite far apart, for your balloon run. The string should be taut.

2 Blow up a balloon with a balloon pump and hold the end to keep the air in. Ask a friend to tape the straw to the balloon.

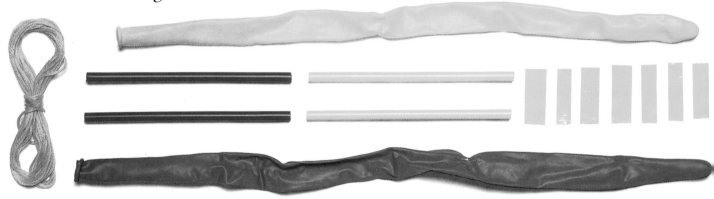

MAKE it WORK!

You can make two models that work in a similar way to a jet engine. The jet balloons allow you to control the thrust produced by high-pressure air escaping from a balloon. You can also make a '**vertical** take off and landing' (VTOL) aircraft which hovers when you provide power by blowing through its straws.

Slide the balloon to one end of the string and let go, so the air can escape. The balloon should whizz along the string to the other end. For further flights, bring the balloon back to the start and blow it up again. The jet balloons work in a similar way to a jet engine. Air thrown out at the back of the balloon pushes the balloon forwards at high speed.

The open neck of the balloon allows air to escape. This propels the balloon forwards along the string.

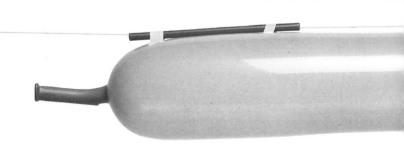

You could set up two strings and have a balloon race. Does twice as much air in the balloon make it go twice as far, or twice as fast?

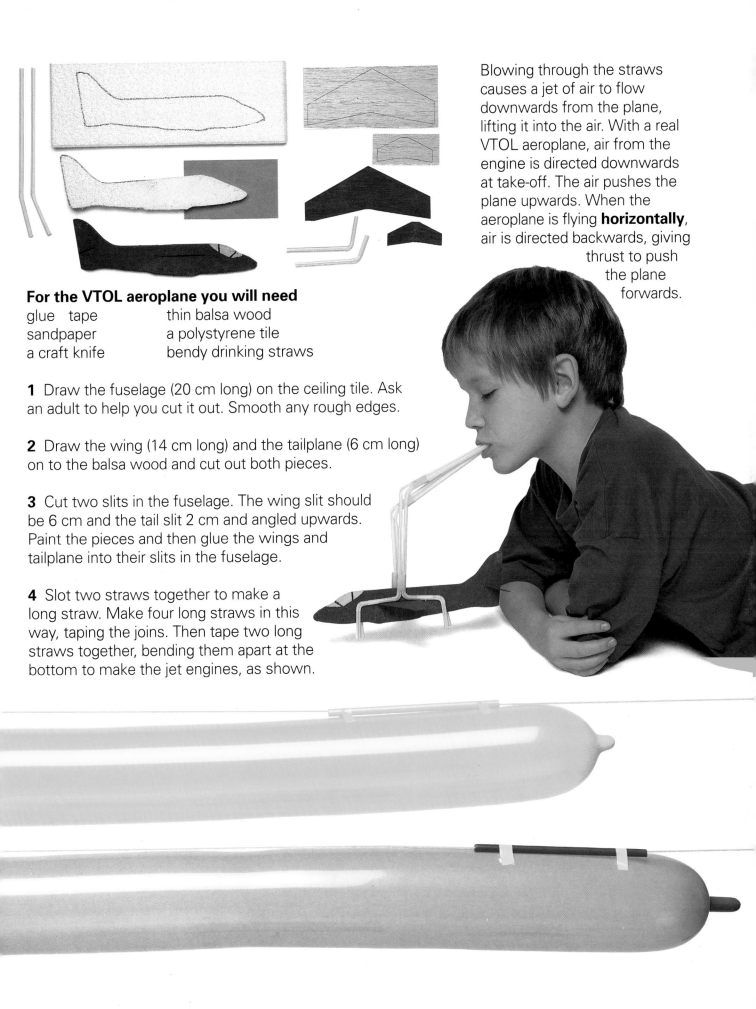

Blowing through the straws causes a jet of air to flow downwards from the plane, lifting it into the air. With a real VTOL aeroplane, air from the engine is directed downwards at take-off. The air pushes the plane upwards. When the aeroplane is flying **horizontally**, air is directed backwards, giving thrust to push the plane forwards.

For the VTOL aeroplane you will need

glue   tape
sandpaper
a craft knife

thin balsa wood
a polystyrene tile
bendy drinking straws

1 Draw the fuselage (20 cm long) on the ceiling tile. Ask an adult to help you cut it out. Smooth any rough edges.

2 Draw the wing (14 cm long) and the tailplane (6 cm long) on to the balsa wood and cut out both pieces.

3 Cut two slits in the fuselage. The wing slit should be 6 cm and the tail slit 2 cm and angled upwards. Paint the pieces and then glue the wings and tailplane into their slits in the fuselage.

4 Slot two straws together to make a long straw. Make four long straws in this way, taping the joins. Then tape two long straws together, bending them apart at the bottom to make the jet engines, as shown.

Rockets are **projectiles** driven by the forward thrust produced when hot gases are forced out of the back of the rocket's engine. The hot gases are produced as rocket fuel burns. This process needs oxygen. Jet engines can use oxygen from the air, but rockets need to carry their own supply because they travel beyond the Earth's atmosphere where there is no air.

You will need

tape	thick card
glue	a paperclip
scissors	a rubber bung
a bradawl	a plastic bottle
carpet tape	a small air valve
	two kitchen roll tubes
	the space shuttle model
	(pages 28 and 29)

MAKE it WORK!

You can make a rocket to launch the space shuttle model described on pages 28 and 29. A space shuttle is helped into orbit by two powerful rocket engines, which separate from the shuttle at a height of about 45 km and parachute back to Earth.

You can try some experiments with your rocket. Does it fly as high if you fill the bottle with water? What happens if you don't put any water in at all?

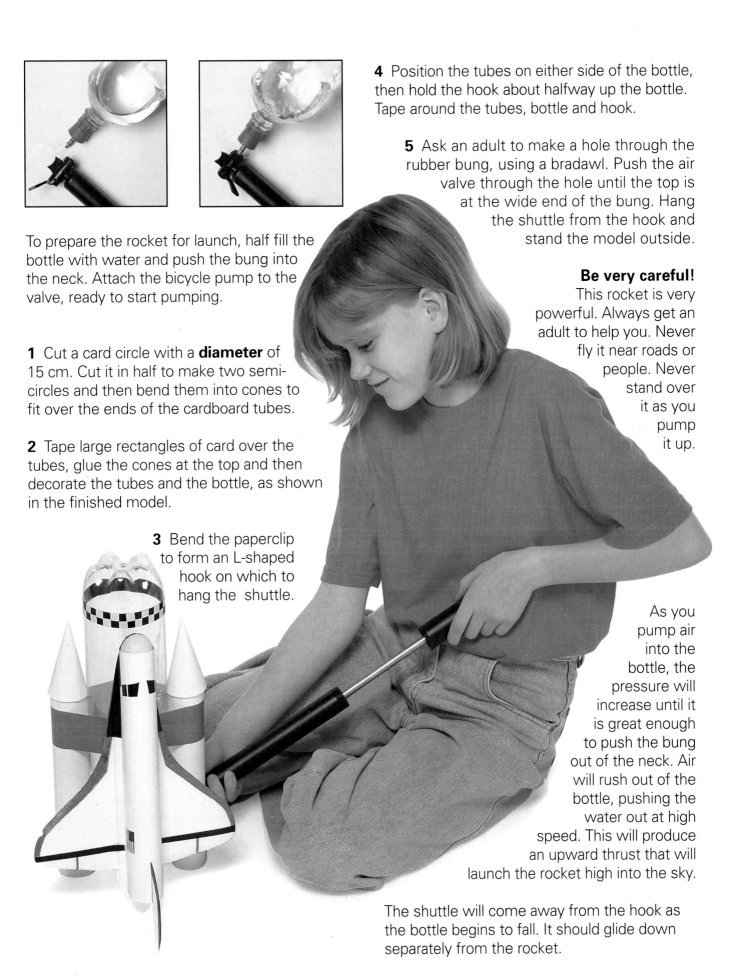

4 Position the tubes on either side of the bottle, then hold the hook about halfway up the bottle. Tape around the tubes, bottle and hook.

5 Ask an adult to make a hole through the rubber bung, using a bradawl. Push the air valve through the hole until the top is at the wide end of the bung. Hang the shuttle from the hook and stand the model outside.

Be very careful!
This rocket is very powerful. Always get an adult to help you. Never fly it near roads or people. Never stand over it as you pump it up.

To prepare the rocket for launch, half fill the bottle with water and push the bung into the neck. Attach the bicycle pump to the valve, ready to start pumping.

1 Cut a card circle with a **diameter** of 15 cm. Cut it in half to make two semi-circles and then bend them into cones to fit over the ends of the cardboard tubes.

2 Tape large rectangles of card over the tubes, glue the cones at the top and then decorate the tubes and the bottle, as shown in the finished model.

3 Bend the paperclip to form an L-shaped hook on which to hang the shuttle.

As you pump air into the bottle, the pressure will increase until it is great enough to push the bung out of the neck. Air will rush out of the bottle, pushing the water out at high speed. This will produce an upward thrust that will launch the rocket high into the sky.

The shuttle will come away from the hook as the bottle begins to fall. It should glide down separately from the rocket.

Aerobatics Spectacular stunts performed in the air. The pilots in aerobatic displays make their aeroplanes twist and turn and do tricks.

Air resistance A force which slows down any object moving through the air. The faster an object moves, the greater the air resistance.

Atmosphere The blanket of air around the Earth. The atmosphere is a mixture of gases. We breathe the lower atmosphere, called the troposphere, which consists of nitrogen (78%), oxygen (21%) and small amounts of argon, water vapour and carbon dioxide.

Banking The way in which an aeroplane turns to the left or right in the air. During banking, the pilot uses the ailerons to roll the aeroplane a little and then uses the rudder to take the aeroplane into a smooth turn.

Control surfaces The parts of an aeroplane which are used to control an aircraft during flight and to help the pilot change direction. There are three main types of control surfaces: ailerons, elevators and rudders.

Density The mass of an object divided by its volume. Polystyrene has a lower density than steel: a block of polystyrene would weigh less than a block of steel of the same size.

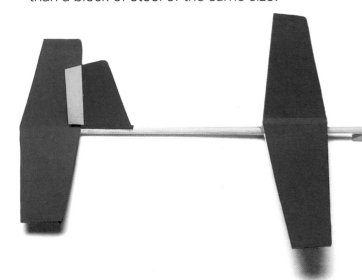

Diameter The distance measured across a circle, passing through the centre.

Drag The air resistance acting on aeroplanes. Drag acts in the opposite direction to thrust.

Energy When something has energy it has the ability to make other things move and change. People use energy stored in their muscles to push and pull loads. Aircraft engines use the energy stored in fuel to provide the thrust needed for flight.

Force A push or pull that is used to lift something, start it moving, or hold it in place against another force, such as gravity. Objects do not have to touch to exert forces on each other. Four forces act on an aeroplane. They are gravity, lift, drag and thrust.

Fuel A substance, such as petrol, burned to produce heat and used to make engines work.

Gravity The force which makes objects fall towards the earth. It is because of gravity that things feel heavy. For an object to fly, an upward force must act upon it to overcome the pull of gravity.

Horizontal Parallel to, or in line with the horizon. Horizontal is the opposite of vertical.

Lift A force which acts upwards against gravity and makes it possible for aeroplanes, airships and balloons to rise in the air.

Mass The amount of matter in a substance, measured in kilograms. The more mass an object has, the more it weighs.

NASA The abbreviation for the National Aeronautics and Space Administration of the United States.

Phenakistoscope A spinning disc used to show moving pictures. A series of images on the disc, when viewed one after the other, give the illusion of movement.

Port The left side of an aeroplane, as seen by the pilot facing the aeroplane's nose.

Power The rate at which something uses energy. An engine with high power uses energy more quickly than a less powerful one, and produces a great deal of thrust.

Pressure The pushing force on a surface.

Projectile An object, such as a cannonball or a rocket, that is thrown forwards and launched into the air.

Radius The distance measured from the centre of a circle to its edge.

Rotate To move around a central point. A propeller rotates around its central hub.

Sonic boom A loud, explosive sound, like a thunderclap, that is caused by the shockwaves an aircraft creates when travelling faster than the speed of sound.

Stability A measure of how hard it is to knock an object off balance.

Starboard The right hand side of an aeroplane, as seen by the pilot when he is sitting in the cockpit facing the nose of the aircraft.

Strain A measure of the force needed to stretch an object.

Strut A solid bar placed between the wings of a biplane to hold them rigid.

Supersonic A supersonic aeroplane, such as Concorde, is one capable of travelling faster than the speed of sound.

Thrust A force that pushes an aeroplane forwards through the air.

Trajectory The curved path that a projectile follows as it travels through the air.

Vertical Perpendicular, or at right angles to the horizon. The opposite of horizontal.

Yaw The way an aeroplane twists to the left and to the right when in flight.